स्लवेस ऑफ़ हैल

शुभांजली निषाद

Made with ♥ on the Notion Press Platform
www.notionpress.com

क्रम-सूची

क्रम-सूची

क्रम-सूची

प्रकाशन के बारे में

वड्र्स ऑफ सोल एक राइटिंग कम्युनिटी है, जहां हमारे पास नए नवोदित लेखकों का एक समूह है, जो भावनाओं को शब्दों में ढालने की अपनी प्रतिभा के साथ हैं।

उत्साही लेखकों को प्रोत्साहित करने और उनकी सराहना करने के लिए 15 मई 2021 को डॉ. निकिता दुदागी और लकी पांडे द्वारा गठित समुदाय के सर्वश्रेष्ठ लेखक को पहचानने के लिए साप्ताहिक विशेष कार्यक्रम और कार्यक्रम आयोजित किए जा रहे हैं। वड्र्स ऑफ सोल, महत्वाकांक्षी लेखकों का एक समूह जो पाठक के मन को प्रेरित करने के लिए अपने दिल की भावनाओं को स्याही करता है।

वड्र्स ऑफ सोल पब्लिकेशन केवल एक प्रकाशन नहीं है, यह लेखकों का एक प्रकार का परिवार है जिसमें सह-लेखक, लेखक, लेखक, संकलक, सह-संकलक, ग्राफिक टीम, परियोजना प्रमुख, सीईओ, सह-संस्थापक और संस्थापक शामिल हैं। यहां हर कोई अपने विचार देने के लिए स्वतंत्र है और हम उनके कार्यों की पहल करते हैं....

प्रस्तावना

स्लवेस ऑफ़ हैल एक ऐसी किताब हैं। जहाँ 29 बेहतरीन लेखकों ने अपने जज़्बातों को कोरे पन्ने पर साँझा किया हैं । खुद को प्रेरित कैसे करें ? कैसे नकारात्मक विचारों से बचे और अपने जीवन में कैसे सफल बने । सकारात्मक विचार से अपने और अपनों का मुश्किलों में साथ निभाकर एक दूसरे के जीवन में एक महत्त्वपूर्ण भूमिका निभाएं ।

आभार

सर्वप्रथम मैं प्रथम पुजनीय गणेश जी के समक्ष नमन करती हूँ । जिनकी कृपा से हमारा यह कार्य बिना किसी बाधा के पूर्ण हो पाया ।उसके बाद मैं अपने माता - पिता का भी दिल से शुक्रिया अदा करती हूँ । मैं "वड्र्स ऑफ़ सोल पब्लिकेशन" के सभी सदस्यों का दिल से आभार व्यक्त करती हूँ । जिन्होंने हम पर विश्वास बनाये रखा और इस सफर में हमारा हौसला बढ़ाया इस किताब में सभी आवश्यक परिवर्तन और बाहरी आवरण को खूबसूरत और आकर्षक बनाने का प्रयास किया ।

अंत में मैं इस मनमोहक पुस्तक "एहसास ए दिल" के पूरे परिवार का तहे दिल से शुक्रिया अदा करती हूँ । जिन्होनें अपना बहुमूल्य समय देकर इस किताब को पूर्ण किया जिनके बिना यह किताब हो पाना कठिन था और इस किताब के समापन में अपना अतुलनीय भूमिका निभाई ।

आप सभी का दिल से आभार

    धन्यवाद

शुभांजली निषाद

1. SHUBHANJALI NISHAD

ये नाम शुभांजली निषाद है इनका जन्म 21 दिसंबर को उत्तर प्रदेश के जिले कानपुर में हुआ था । वा इन्होंने अपनी शिक्षा सीजेएसएम

यूनिवर्सिटी से पूर्ण की है इनको लिखने का काफी शौक वा इनकी रुचि हिंदी काव्य लेखन में भी है अथवा यह इस पुस्तक "SLAVES OF HELL" की संकलन कर्ता भी है । वह 500+ से अधिक संकलनों में सह-लेखक के तौर पर भाग ले चुकी हैं और उन्होंने दो संकलन भी किये हैं इनकी पहली संकलन पुस्तक का नाम "किसान" और दूसरे संकलन का नाम "फीलिंग्स ऑफ हार्ट" था । इन्हें लिखने के साथ ही पुस्तके पढ़ने वा नई जगहों पर घूमना भी अधिक पसंद करती हैं ।

वह सभी प्रकार की कविताएं लिखने में रुचि रखती है । और उन्हें कल्पनाओं में भ्रमण करना पसंद है उन्हीं कल्पना पर मदद के माध्यम से ये अपने विचारों को कोरे पन्नों में अपनी रचनाओं को खूबसूरती से लिखने कि हुनर रखतीं हैं और इन्होंने अपनी कविता लेखन की माध्यम से कयी रोज़ाना काव्य प्रतियोगिता में भाग लिया है एवं ये कयी प्रतियोगिता में विजय भी हुई है ।

जिंदगी की नयी शुरूआत

बहुत जी लिया उदास मन से मैंने

अब जिंदगी को खुश मन से जीना

चाहती हूं मैं जैसी चल रही है जिदंगी

मेरी उसमें कुछ बदलाव लाना चाहती

हूं मैं जिंदगी के हर सिरे को मजबूती से

पकड़ अपने जिंदगी की बागडोर को नयी

दिशा दिखाना चाहती हूं मै जो हुआ है पिछले

दिनों में उन सब बातों को भूल एक नयी तरह

से हमेशा खुशहाल जीवन बिताना चाहती हूं मै ।

हर दिन मै जिंदगी को नये ढंग से जीना चाहती हूं

गुजरती पीढ़ियों की पंरपरा को नयी पीढ़ी के संग

हर चीज को सहजता से ढालना चाहती हूं हर दिन

जिंदगी के पलों को हंसीन लम्हों में बदलना चाहती हूं ।

2. AMB. MAID CORBIC

Maid Corbic from Tuzla, 22 years old. In his spare time he writes poetry that repeatedly praised as well as rewarded. He also selflessly helps others around him, and he is moderator of the World Literature Forum WLFPH (World Literature Forum Peace and Humanity) for humanity and peace in the world in Bhutan. He is also the editor of the First Virtual Art portal led by Dijana Uherek Stevanovic. Many works have also been published in anthologies and journals (Chile, Spain,

Ecuador, Bosnia and Herzegovina, San Salvador, United Kingdom, Indonesia).

A SLAVE OF THE HELL OF THE WORLD

Hell is brewing in my womb and heart

When I see finches how you are with another

So my heart beats more and more

Because I'm afraid you're leaving

You from me forever

I am only the posen link of life

But I am afraid to remain sad still

Just because I feel needed

At least to myself if not to others

And I have to go ahead strongly

It is better for me to be a slave to hell

Because when love turns all memories

I'm just looking for you, but you're gone

So what should I do with my destiny?

I have to trust only myself really

And I can build my life the way I want

Only time is on my side

And the meaning of life for me is

Just to believe from today to tomorrow

Faith and hope that I am not a slave to hell

What a life without you, my dear

When every memory of you reminds me

And my silence which is present in the heart

She doesn't come back anymore

Because silence is gold today!

3. DR.ERAM ANWAR

She is Dr.Eram Anwar, last year she has completed her Dentistry. She has kin interest in writing poems on different genres specially the philosophical one. She loves to maintain journal, read non fictious books and create imagination. Her dreams are to write and write and write and become an absolutely appreciable Author along with being a Doc.

MASSACRE

Time ere were ecstatic I was a wholesome being with a blossoming heart, working brain, and glorifying skin.

A very tiny piece of me is left now, now I'm a person with shrunken skin, truncated and rusted mind and a heart who needs a permanent cardioversion to beat.

Protecting the residual me is not easy because the pray is in love with the slayer,

Bewitching! Literally.

Else every cell and nerve and muscle are verily consumed after being cachexic unnaturally but intentionally by those philanthropists who's ocean full of love were not for me.

How enthralling it could be, if a lover is being prepared for slaughtering by none other than his beloved, who seems the whole world to her. How much devastation and brokenness a person is carring who has started contemplating and arranging such massacre for herself eventually.

It's not that I have forgotten the meaning of dazzlement, although I have kissed my misfortune and kneeled in front of it.

Dr. Eram

4. CHANDNI BAID

The author name is Chandni Baid. Her pen and writings are all about connecting the feelings with each reader heart, and to make readers feel like home. She writes, what she feels, experiences and emotions she lives.

पहली नज़र में जिंदगी

पहली नज़र में जिंदगी वार दी उस पर

वो मौत एक हसीन बला थी

सामने खडी मुस्कुरा रहीं थी, इतरा रही थी

मानों मुझ्से मुझे मांग रही थी

वो आंखो में उसका यू शिद्दत से देखना

मानों मुझे अपनी अदाओं से रिझा रही थी

वो उसका पल पल मेरे करीब आना

मानों मेरी सांसे होलेहोले लेजा रही थी

और फिर आकर मुझे अपनी बाहों में भर लेना

मानों मुझे अपने मोहब्बत में पिघला रही थी !!

और फिर उसके छूते ही , यूं वक्त का रुक जना

मानों मेरे रूह को कायनात की सैर करा रही थी!!

कायनात तक नहीं बच पाई इसके हुस्न से

वो मौत एक हसीन बला थी !!

5. MURALIDHAR BANSAL

HE IS MURALIDHAR BANSAL FROM NEPAL HE LOVES WRITING AND STARTED WRITING WHEN HE WAS A STUDENT. PLAYING CRICKET AND WRITING ARE HIS HOBBIES .

खुद से मोहब्बत

कुछ पल में बिखरता हूँ

बिखरने से ही में निखरता हूँ।

हर रोज नई-नई कहानी लिखता हूँ

कर्योंकि तुझसे पहले में खुद को देखता हूँ ।।

हर मुकाम के लिए आज में लड़ता हूँ

कभी में पीछे नहीं हटता हूँ ।

तुझसे कहने मे यह नहीं डरता हूँ

कर्योंकि में खुद को ही प्रेरित करता हूँ ।।

शिखर है आगे, उस ओर में बढता हूँ

एक एक सफलता की सीडी में चढता हूँ ।

तुम आज भी सोचती हो कि में तुम्हारे लिए आहे भरता हूँ

तुम गलत हो, में अब खुद से मोहब्बत करता हूँ ।।

6. ADRIANA ROCHA

Adriana Rocha was born in Bolivia. She is a psychologist who teaches English to business administration, odontology, medicine and law students. Poetry, photography and educational psychology are her passions. Her journey into the world of words has started in 2019. She has been participating in different literary events in Latin America, Spain and India.

He'll

She was meant to go to heaven,

But she chose to go to hell,

To dance among the fire flames.

***

I kissed a man

I kissed a man

When I was going to hell,

I said why not,

Perhaps down there

I will not have another chance.

7. ROHIT RAJ

He is student cum newcomer writer who is mostly interested towards poetry and is still to start his story writing journey.

तू संघर्ष करता चल ......

क्यों आजकल तू

यूँ रोता सा रहा है

हाथों पे हाथ डाले

आखिर क्यों तू

हथियार डाले पड़ा है

मुसीबतों का आना

होता रहा है

आखिर क्यों तू उनसे

घबराता रहा है

तेरी आँखें क्यूँ

इतनी रोती अधिक है

क्यों भावनाओं के समुद्र में

तू डूबता रहा है

चल, उठ , ज़रा कोशिश कर ले

क्यों हालातों को दोषी

तू ठहराता रहा है

पहचान कर ले

अपनी शक्तियों की

क्यों खुद को तू निर्बल

बताता रहा है

लाख चुनौतियां आयेंगी

तू टकरा जाना उनसे

हौसले की एक

मजबूत दीवार बनकर

तेरे दम से होगी

तेरी ख्वाहिशें पूरी

बस बढ़ते जाना

अपने सफर पर

विश्वास के घोड़े पर सवार

बिलकुल एक घुड़सवार बनकर ।

8. DEYA RAJIV MUKHERJEE

She is Deya Rajiv Mukherjee, a girl from West Bengal, India. She is currently a graduation student of 6th semester at South Calcutta Girls' College, Kolkata and her Honours subject is Sociology Honours. Her hobbies include listening to music and writing. She is also a co - author in many anthologies.

JOURNEY

Life is a very difficult journey and during the path of this journey, we have to face different kinds of situations and meet different people. Some people whom we meet in life are good, humble and who want us to always stay happy. On the contrary, there are some people who don't like us and just hate us . So , a key factor by which you can overcome any situation or problem is self motivation. If you have belief in yourself and in your ability and work , everything is possible. But , nothing can be achieved if we don't have self motivation.

We may feel hopeless in some situations and it's normal. But , in such cases, remember not to lose hope and have belief in yourself. Struggles and difficulties are all parts of everyone's life but having believe on your own self makes you to move forward and achieve higher success. This is what makes you different from others in every aspect .

Also remember that life never stops, it goes on and on. Life stops only when we think it has stopped. People who face every situation and try to overcome them are the real heroes as they can achieve their goals and everything they want only with their will power and self motivation and determination.

That's why, never feel that you are incapable of overcoming the situations. But instead, think that you will be able to cross every hurdle that comes in your way just with your inner strength and self motivation.

Thus , self motivation is the key to a successful life without which no one can achieve anything.

9. SHRISTHI SINGH

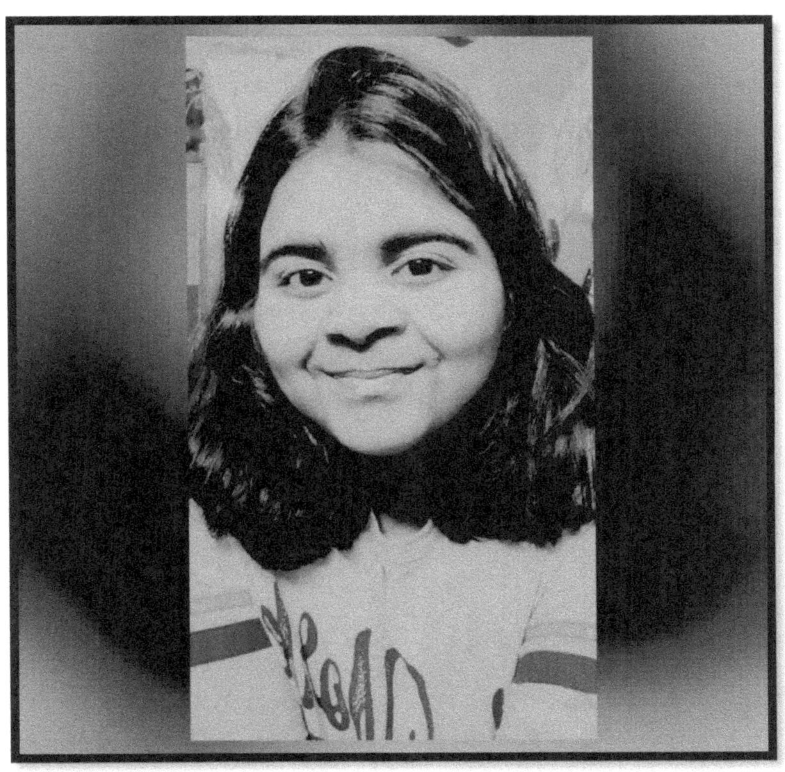

Shrishti singh is a 15 year old young poetess from Ghatotand, Jharkhand. She loves to express herself through poetry . Shrishti says " Poetry is something I love to do when I'm happy , sad , furious, curious or something else. There were many people who said to stop because I was growing up and as I've entered tenth standard , they were forcing me to stop . But as a my dad always calls me an ocean , so ocean can't be controlled by any human it can only be controlled by God. So I didn't stopped writing even though they asked me to do so". She also says that "If you've the courage to do multiple tasks then believe me you're the strongest person in the World".

STAND

Stand , For what you believe in ,

Stand ,For what you love ,

You can just try to fit in ,

So Stand , to remind everyone what's your worth .

We fall in love to hard to fast ,

And then there's our broken heart at last,

Why can't we love ourselves the same way ,

Why can't we appreciate ourselves everyday?

So just stand , for who you are ,

Stand , you've drift very far .

You're so much more than what the world thinks ,

Try to improve yourself so the next time you don't stink.

We all have got so many differences ,

But it's on us how we break the ice ,

We all have some fences between us ,

But we can work it out , right guys?

So just stand , for yourself

So just stand , to be better than everybody else.

Yep we fall in love with someone who doesn't loves us
back ,

And then we assume that they're so bad,

But when we set our differences aside ,

And then they're the once who put us back on the right
track.

10. JUGESH SINGH THAKUR

Jugesh Singh Thakur is an Indian author and poet .Hails from pogal and paristan valley of Ramban district (Jammu and Kashmir) . Jugesh Singh Thakur believes that writing is a soul healer it dilutes the quality of depression. Besides writing he loves singing, researching and motivating others. He has been the author of 'The Craved Emotions". Author at Profound writers, And co-author of more than 20 anthologies

जीतना जीवन का आधार नहीं!

मान गया कि मैं जीत न पाया

पर यह ना समझना कि मैं थक हार गया!

हारना तो है ही जीवन के सफर में

पर यह न समझना कि मैं कोशिश करना छोड़ गया!

हार के डर से मैंने अपना रास्ता नहीं मोड़ा

हां मैं अब उनके जैसे बहाने ढूंढना छोड़ गया!

कुछ गलतियों की वजह से मैंने हार मान ली थी

पर यह ना समझना कि मैं सीखना छोड़ गया!

गलत तो हूं नहीं कि मैं मुश्किलों का सामना नहीं करता

गलत तो मैं तब होता जब अपना रास्ता मोड़ लेता!

जिंदगी क्या है, हार के बाद ही तो जीत है

पर यह ना समझना , कि जितना ही जीवन का आधार है!

अब तो मंजिल की राह हमवार नजर आती है जुगेश

जो अब मेरी सफलता से,जमाना भी जलने लगा!

जुगेश सिंह ठाकुर.

जम्मू कश्मीर

11. RANBIR BHAKAT

Author by heart and passion.Writing since He was 16. Ranbir Bhakat is pursuing an integrated undergraduate course in Commerce from Calcutta University, Kolkata. He was born and brought up in Kolkata, West Bengal. His writeups touches reality and reaches everyone's heart. After publishing his own book he wants to explore more. He wants to grasp and grow in his writing journey.

Gmail: ranbirbhakat5456@gmail.com

Insta Id: @_writing__tales_

I WASN'T ALONE

For most of my life, I've been on a quest

To discover just who I might be,

Earnestly searching, day after day,

So desperate to recognize me.

I've felt moments of utter fulfillment

And moments I couldn't go on,

But I knew for the sake of my heart and my soul,

To succeed, I would have to be strong.

But the people around me seemed so lost themselves

That I feared I might be on my own.

But then there'd be someone who would reach out and help

And remind me I wasn't alone.

12. SHIWANI TIWARI

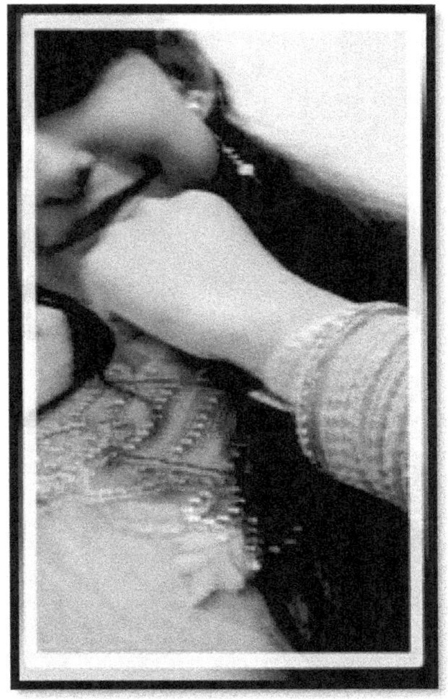

She is Shiwani tiwari from Delhi and graduate from
DU.
Love to spend time with family and friends.playing with
kids and love to play tennis.

भ्रष्टाचार

भ्रष्टाचार इतना बढ़ गया है लोगों के दिल में डर बैठ गया है,

नेता के खिलाफ आवाज उठाते हैं तो परिवार को मारने की धमकी देते हैं
नेता,,

जो आवाज़ न उठाए वो खुद नरक का दरवाज़ा खोलते हैं,,

नरक का दरवाज़ा खोलकर खुद नाराज के गुलाम बनते हैं,,

पता है जब जुल्म सहना अत्याचार है,,

तो क्यों तुम करते ऐसा व्यवहार हो,,

चलो आवाज़ उठाओ इस भ्रष्टाचार के खिलाफ,,

हम नहीं बनेंगे नरक के गुलाम।

13. MARIA SHAIKH

Maria Shaikh, a passionate writer from Jajpur, Odisha. She is the daughter of Sk Lal Mohammed and Husn Ara. She believes in living life before life turns its way from enjoyment to a harshness. She writes Quotes, Short Shayari, Poems, and Articles. She worked as a co- author in 15+ books. She has compiled a book named *Quarantine 2020*.

She was featured in TZP as a VOICEBREAKER. She has her fame in Daily hunt and medium news.

KHUD SE MILTE HAI

Aao Jara khud se milte Hain

Khud ki baat ham khud hi se karte Hain

Duniyadari to bahut ho gai

Ab waqt sochne ki khud ki aayi

Har waqt pyar Mohabbat Chand Tare mein ulajhte Hain

Aaj waqt hamara hai chalo khud per kuchh likhte Hain

Yun Mohabbat To humne sabse ki hai

Aaj khud ko dekh kar khud Ko samajhne ki bari aayi hai

Akshar hum bhul jaate hain, hume humaari v jrurt hai,

Hum kyun apni jrurt puri nhi krte hain,

Puri duniya ko to hum badi chah se niharte hain,

Khudka khayal hum kyun nhi rakh paate Hain,

Hume pata hai, hum koi jaadugar nhi,

Phir v apni jindagi uljhi hui kyun chod dete hain,

Jindagi jeena to humara v haq hai,

Wo haq humesha hum kyun dusron ko de dete hain,

Yun to hum dusron ki tareef badi khushi se karte hain,

Phir aayena me dekhkr khud ko kyun bhala bura kehte hain,

Ye waqt humaara hai janaab, ise jaya na karo,

Khudko dusron se mawajne se pehle, apne andar to jhaank liya karo...

14. ANAM RIZVI

Anam Rizvi, Lucknow is a certified teacher with Basic Teaching Certificate. She is a science graduate pursuing MSc Mathematics. Her interest lies in writing poems and painting.

JABKI SAPNE JAG RAHE

Haasil har ek chiz ho pr,

Uth na tak muhaal lage.....

Besud or gumrah hn jo,

Jada garmi kaat rhe....

Kaise inki ankhe band hn,

Jbki sapne jaag rhe!..

Mehnatkash ko qismat kehkar,

Apna ghm h chupa rhe....

Afsos bahane ilzaam liye,

Kch soch soch kr haar rhe....

Kaise inki ankhe band hn,

Jbki sapne jaag rhe!..

Chlo man liya tm kahil ni,

Ye man liya koi sath nhi...

Khud aap me apne kafi ho,

Sapne tmhi to dekhe ho ....

Kaise tb bhi ankhe bnd hn,

Jabki sapne jaag rhe! ..

Insan ho rona aega,

Dr bhi tmko sataega….

Kuch sunna pdega sunte rho,

Chukane ko qeemat tyyar rho…

Naa jane kaise ankhe bnd hn,

Jbki sapne jaag rhe!...

awaz suno koi bula rha,

Ankhe kholo koi jaga rha..

Ye hqiqat bnna chahte hn,

Ye tumme jeena chahte hn…

Inko tmse aas bdi h,

Dekho mnzil pas khadi h…

Abi ka wqt bda saral h,

Age jeewan bda jatil h…

In ankho ne, h dekha jo bhi,

Poora vo sb kr jao…

Lad jao ya mr jao,

Jo bhi karna kr jao….

Baith baith socho na,

Jo socha h pa jao….

Inki jbtk nhi sunoge,

Aj se behtr ni bnoge….

Karlo pyar inhise tum,

Pyar se zda paoge….

Duniabhr k sare rishte,

Daud k khud_hi aege….

Gr zinda ho to pura karo,

Murdo jaise bs palo na….

Sbkch kahn h sabke pas,

Par sabko sbkch bula rha….

Tumhare jaisi zndgi bhi,

Duao me koi h mang rha….

Ek dafa jo chah gae dono,

Mumkin sb ho skta h....

Ek "tum" or "sapne" se,

Bqi jeewan sudhar sakta h....

Phir kaise ab bhi ankhe band hn?

Jbki sapne jaag rhe hn....

~Anam_Rizvi♥

15. JASWALINI BARAL

She is Jaswalini Baral.she is an engineering graduate. She used to live in Bhubaneswar city of Odisha. She used to acquire knowledge from different kinds of skills. Her main motive is to spread happiness.

MEIN HUN APNI SAHARA

Manzilein na raah ki talaash thi,

Jahan dekhti thi bas andhera chayi hui thi.

Har mod par har koi bas taane ke upar taane sunata raha,

Har koi bas mujhe aage badhne par mere paon khich ke
rokta tokta raha.

Khushiyan jese meri kho si gayi,

Dukh ka pahad jese mujhpe gir si gayi.

Fir bhi mein haar naa mani,

Mujhe duniya se kya lena hai,

Khudke liye mujhe khade rehna hai yehi jazbaat ko mein
ne thaani.

Andheron mein humein khud nikal ke roshni dhudhna hai,

Duniya ke baat ko naa darte huye bas aage badhte jaana
hai.

Aj jo log taana thokte hai mujhpe unhi ko chupi karana hai,

Kuch aisa kar dikha kar unhi ko kamiyaabi dikhana hai.

Maidaan ran bhumi ka ho zindagi ka,

Khel jesa bhi ho zindagi ka,

Humein jeet ke aage nikalna hai.

16. NANDINI BANSAL

Nandini is a teenager living in uttarakhand.
She has been exploring the enchanted world of poetry
since she was 14. Giving words to thoughts is
something she loves the most.

A Dreamy Sky

Covered with blanket of stars,

Shining from the far,

This beautiful night took my heart.

While yearning to see the sunrise,

Got myself stuck in this glazy night,

And couldn't get my eyes off from this sight.

Sitting along the seashore was so amazing,

Can't explain my feeling,

My eyes were shimmering.

The cold breeze was so relaxing,

That made me feel if I was imagining,

The feeling was so overwhelming.

It seems it was a dream,

That faded with the daytime,

Wishing to see again that night.

17. भावना विधानी

अमरावती निवासी सौभाग्यवती भावना मोहन कुमार विधानी को बचपन से ही लेखन का बहुत शौक रहा है। उन्होंने अपने लेखन का सफर कक्षा सातवीं से बाल कविताओं के रूप में शुरू किया। उन्होंने अब तक काफी सारे लेख शायरी कहानियां कविताएं लिखी है, जो काफी सारी पत्र-पत्रिकाओं में प्रकाशित हो चुकी है। उन्होंने कई बार ऑनलाइन कवि सम्मेलनों में भाग लिया है। लेखन के साथ-साथ भावना जी को बागवानी कुकिंग और गायन का शौक है।

जिन्दगी के कुछ रंग ऐसे भी

जीवन ऐसा रंगीन ख्वाब देखो सदा हसीन,

दुख हो या सुख रोना ना कभी रखना सदा होठों पर हंसी।

जीवन रथ चलता जाये दुख के बाद सुख ही आये,

जीवन होगा खुशियां वाला प्रभु सदा ही है रखवाला।

जीवन के कुछ रंग ऐसे भी खुशियां ले आते हैं कैसे भी,

जीवन की हर परिस्थिति को करो सलाम,

महफूज रखो सितारों में अपना नाम।

सौ, भावना विधानी

18. DR.CHANDRESH KUMAR CHHATLANI

Dr. Chandresh Kumar Chhatlani has over 25 years of rich experience in Training, Research, Academics, Writing, Software Development, Website Development and Design Developed more than 140 software & websites independently). He is a record holder for earning highest academic certificates from World's Greatest Records. Dr. Chhatlani has adequate experience of all types of documentation and dealing with NAAC Assessment, UGC, AICTE, MHRD, NIRF,

Distance Education, AISHE, Supreme Court, PCI, CCH etc.

AM AWAY FROM AWAY FROM MYSELF

I'm imperfect

Yet I am the only one.

I am with my own approval,

But am insufficient.

I know that

That immutable is contained in me

But I am deformative and changeable.

With the power of creation

I am the lord of the supernatural.

Yet every particle of blood

I have to purify.

It's impossible for divinity to cut me

There is no need for anything else.

With a tendency to accumulate things,

How am I abundant, thoughts are silent.

I am the source of all joy,

I am beyond every moment of every disorder.

But I convert the energy of the universe

Into happiness and sorrow.

I never look in the mirror

Can't see myself

Self realization is salvation

Why do I walk away from myself ?

19. ESHA GUPTA

Esha Gupta, native of Haldaur, district Bijnor (U.P.), currently pursuing Bachelor of Science in Mathematics(hons). She loves writing and her thought provoking mind always inspires her to write more & more. Apart from writing, she loves crafting and photography. She is an active participant in different poetry contests. She has been a part of about seventeen anthologies yet.

मोटिवेशन कोई छुट्टी नहीं

किसी भी इंसान को मोटिवेशन

का असर तब तक नहीं होग,

जब तक उसमें कुछ कर जाने के

जज़्बे का जन्म स्वयं नहीं होग,

बार-बार आ रही असफलताओं

का स्वीकार उसे ही करना होगा,

सफलता की पहली सीढ़ी

असफलता को उसे ही चूमना होगा,

रास्ते में आई परेशानियों का

उसे डट कर सामना करना ही होगा,

इंसान अगर चाहे तो

क्या कुछ नहीं होगा,

उसे खुद की ही प्रेरणा बन

अपना मार्गदर्शन करना होगा !!

20. BANASO KUMARI

Banaso Kumari is 17 year old student from jharkhand.She love to write.She is free spirit and nature lover.She love to write to express her hidden feelings.She believe that writing is directly connected to heart and is better to express emotions. She have a such a creativity that she can write anything connected to real life and emotions.....she is little sensitive girl,she writes all her poems getting lesson from her life.She is a author of her solo book also...tooo she is co-author in more than 100 books.

मुसाफिर आगे बढ़ते चलो

राह में मुस्किल होगी हजार,तुम दो कदम बढ़ाओ तो सही।

मुस्किले पर इतनी नहीं की तुम कर न सको।

दूर है मंजिल लेकिन इतनी भी नहीं की तुम पा ना सको।

तुम चलो तो सही तुम चलो तो सही।

तुम दो कदम बढ़ाओ तो सही ,हो जाए गा सपना साकार।

एक दिन तुम्हारा भी नाम होगा,

तुम्हारा भी सत्कार होगा।

तुम कुछ लिखो तो सही,

तुम कुछ आगे पढ़ो तो सही।

तुम चलो तो सही,तुम चलो तो सही।

सपनो के सागर मैं कब तक गोता लगाते रहो गए?

तुम्हारे पास एक रह है चुनो तो सही।

तुम उठो तो सही ,तुम कुछ करो तो सही।

तुम चलो तो सही,तुम चलो तो सही

कुछ ना मिले तो कुछ सीख जाओगे,

जिंदगी का अनुभव साथ ले जाओगे।

गिरते पड़ते संभाल जाओगे,

फिर एक बार तुम भी जीत जाओगे।

21. JEET VERMA

Jeet Verma from Jharkhand and I write poem not to feel lonely because some emotions you can't share but you can share with your pen and paper. Poem is not only a poem but it is a way to express your feelings your emotions and to change the mind set of people and makes this world a better place to live.

SPEECHLESS

A tears of quietness

A tears of being speechless

Being speechless after getting cheated by everyone

Being speechless after getting ruined for my Body

Being speechless after getting laugh on my dream and idea

Being speechless after not getting support from parents

Being speechless as I am walking alone in

My dream path

Being speechless because I have faith on Myself

Being speechless because one you all will be speechless

After seeing my shine of success

But, for now I am speechless…

22. Prajwal K.M.

Prajwal K.M. who is a student, poet and writer in Kannada and English languages. Who is from the malenadu region of hassana district that is 'Poor's Ootie' Sakleshpura. Presently serving as a district organizing secretary in "Sirigannada Vedike". Also a motivational speaker who gives free sessions without any cost.

Contact number : 8217553829

Insta ID : Prajwal alpha

MY EYES WERE BLINKING

Mighty soul,

I still blinking my eyes,

To infinitive thoughts I have,

In the fear of dark days,

That might long live.

Nature on nurturing itself

Posed a situation,

We dismay.

With courage boost yourself,

Let all frustration go away

Problem isn't lead us ever

But I'm still blinking my eyes

For the light of hope forever

At which darkness never

Stays.

Still I'm blinking the eyes,

Deeming at the cloudless sky

And waiting for the sun to

Rise Where he brings the

Enormous joy.

My God,

Shower your mercy on us

Often we live life well

Why this sorrow been in

Cause? When you end, Oh!

Lord please tell

Im in dark, bring me into light

Here im blinking my eyes to Unknown.

Prajwal K.M. Sakaleshapura.

THE ENDLESS

It may be late, the beginning

I know if you initiate your journey

None can stop you in your way

It may be hard, the way you walking

I know you will stil strive diligently

Where your sadness dismay

And you will reach at the destiny

Which is eternal and you are humble

For sure you will reach to the top of all

Which is heaven for your folks

How much restless nights

And the sunny dark days

But the day will come with happy home

Till that run and run and run

Never stop till the aim come

And end where heavenly nymphs welcomes

At instant you shun the slaves of the hell

Which pinched to supress you in the well

And bring the season of happiness

To the home we dwell,,,,,, Oo Dear..

23. RITU

Name of co-author is Ritu. She hailing from delhi.Her Passion is a writing and hobbies is reading and travelling... Her aim is to achieve success in a short time.

She want to become a professional writer in his life she completed 50+ anthology books as a co author contact with her through Gmail rituk5178@gmail.com

A GIRL BEHIND ME

A girl behind me

Laughs with many,

Happy with nobody,

She smiles randomly,

Who knows!

She screeme so badly ,

A girl behind me

Lock her face within the pillow,

Saying everything's all right ,

The reality she lock her pain and cry all night

A girl behind me

Says she don't care,

The world says she's rock hearted

Who's knows!

She broken inside.

24. MRUNMAYI DHAGE

Mrunmayi Dhage She is from Mumbai She is known as Graphologist
vedic math teacher numerologist
handwriting teacher poet writer drawing analysis
Author Handwriting Expert Signature Expert Social worker.

HAND OF LIFE

Ere yet this hand a life of torment close,

And end by one determin'd stroke my woes,

Is there a fond regret, which moves my mind

To pause, and cast a ling'ring look behind?

—O my lov'd bride!—for I have call'd thee mine,

Dearer than life, whom I with life resign,

For thee ev'n here this faithful heart shall glow,

A pang shall rend me, and a tear shall flow.—

How shall I soothe thy grief, since fate denies

Thy pious duties to my closing eyes?

I cannot clasp thee in a last embrace,

Nor gaze in silent anguish on thy face;

I cannot raise these fetter'd arms for thee,

To ask that mercy heav'n denies to me;

Yet let thy tender breast my sorrows share,

Bleed for my wounds, and feel my deep despair.

Yet let thy tears bedew a wretch's grave,

Whom fate forbade thy tenderness to save.

Receive these sighs—to thee my soul I breathe—

Fond love in dying groans is all I can bequeathe.

25. CHANCHAL GUPTA

@hamari___soch is her insta I'd you can follow on Instagram ,my name is chanchal gupta, She is a student

अकेले चलना सीखा है

हर राह पर अकेले चलना सीखा है हमने ,

हर मुश्किल से खुद ही लड़ना सिखा है हमने,

राह मैं मिले तो बहुत से लोग,

लेकिन सबको साथ छोड़ते देखा है हमने,

हर राह पर अकेले चलना सीखा है हमने हर मुश्किल से खुद ही लड़ना सिखा है ,

वादा करके मुकरते देखा है हमने,

हर किसी को रंग बदलते देखा है हमने,

हर राह पर अकेले चलना सिखा है हमने।

26. GANGABAI B NEGINAL

She is being a techincal student. she is fascinated in literature in kannada, English, Hindi language.And over all I wrote hundred plus poems and quotes.

SLAVES OF HELL

Don't be a slave in heaven be a king/queen in hell.Hell is empty here because devils are here.why we are going to became salves of hell? No, I cant I am becoming queen of the hell. Because hell is not bad place that is also good place like heaven how we are thinking. Hell is like a heaven when we thinking postivity in life. We are not customers, we are not labours in hell. We are owner and that is our kingdom and we are the king and queen in hell not salves of hell.

27. NEELAKSH

Neelaksh hails from Lucknow, Uttar Pradesh. He has completed his B.com from Jai Narayan pg college and is pursuing Chartered Accountant. He usually writes as a part of his hobby. He express himself beautifully and love to write on different occasions . He always tries to bring smiles to everyone face.. He is always hopeful and bring positive memories to others

SLAVERY... A CURSE

All on that charming coast is no bitter .

Fair Freedom

And I think on friends most dear, with the bitter, bitter tear

The scourge that drove the laborer to the field..

In scary night I wandered, praying,

Lord God my harshener,

Sudden brightness clove the preying

Darkness, brightness that was

Some view our sable race with scornful eye

Taught my benighted soul to understand

That there's a God, that there' Savior too.

28. ATHARV PATIL

Amigo. This is Atharv Patil, a 19 year old college going boy, just hustling to get something best our of his life.

OPPORTUNITY TO GROW

Everyday…..

Waking up to the same lies,

Everyday…..

A part of me dies..

But it's up to you,

To sit alone, and to cry…

Or just with a smile

Spread your wings, and to fly…

It's not a chance, but my choice.

Just listen to your own voice….

It's important to love yourself

At times you are your best help….

Life is a beautiful gift… It's just how you see it . The same pain that give you a scar teaches you how to be strong and be a shining star.. The same problem is a trouble as well as an opportunity to grow….

29. ANMOL DAVE

Anmol Dave, is a resident of Uttar Pradesh. he has completed BA degree . she is really passionate about writing and have achieved certificate of participation, E- certificate and E- trophy in various anthologies organized by various communities.

LOVE YOURSELF

You are here to discover something amazing about you

If you will love yourself in a

Manner like no one have ever

Loved you then you will

Discover something really

Amazing about yourself

That no one have ever

Told you.

There will be a day you will

Do something really incredible

In your life that no one have

Ever imagined nor you have ever

Imagined about you, because

You are here to discover

Something amazing

About you.

30. ACHARYA ASHISH PANDEY

आचार्य आशीष पाण्डेय १२-७-२०००-सुल्तानपुर उत्तर प्रदेश के परसडा नामक ग्राम में हुआ है इनकी बचपन से ही काव्य में रुचि रही जिसके फलस्वरूप इन्होंने २०वर्ष की अवस्था में पुस्तकों की रचना की, विभिन्न पत्रिकाओं में इनकी रचना प्रकाशित हुई है और आगे भी होती रहेगी।ये काव्य भारती, सरस्वती सृजन सम्मान,युवा,शक्ति, सरदार वल्लभ भाई पटेल जैसे आदि पुरस्कारों से सम्मानित हैं

ये अभी अध्ययन रत है और भागवत कथा कर्मकाण्ड,ज्योतिष आदि के जानकार भी हैं

ये अभी अध्ययन रत है और भागवत कथा कर्मकाण्ड,ज्योतिष आदि के जानकार भी हैं

इश्वर की आराधना करना

नर्क का गुलाम बनने से अच्छा है

थोड़ा कष्ट सहकर पृथ्वी पर

ईश्वर की आराधना कर उद्धार पाना।

क्योंकि नर्क के गुलामों की हालत कैसी है

ये क्या बताऊं

बस इतना जानो

नर्क शब्द से ही उसकी पहचान हो जाती है।।

वहां का जीवन पृथ्वी के जीवन से

अधिक गुना ज्यादा कष्ट दायी है

इसलिए ईश्वर की आराधना कर

उद्धार करो उद्धार करो।।

© आचार्य आशीष पाण्डेय

31. ANTARA CHOUDHURY

अंतरा चौधरी, नागपुर महाराष्ट्र की निवासी हैं । वह पिछले कुछ सालों से लिख रही हैं। उन्हें लिखने का शौक हैं ।उन्हें भ्रमण करना भी बहुत पसंद है । वह कहती हैं की जज़्बातों को लिखकर ज़ाहिर करने से दिल को सुकून मिलता हैं और लिखकर दिल की बात ज़ाहिर करना भी एक कला हैं। उन्हें पढ़ना और लिखना दोनों पसंद हैं । उन्होंने 50+ अन्थोलोजी एवं 1 डुओ किताब में काम किया है और 4 किताबें संकलक के तौर पर आ चुकी है ।

वो खुद को खुशनसीब मानती हैं की वह बहुत ही सरल भाषा में

लिखती हैं ताकि सब पढ़ सकें।
संपर्क करने हेतु - इंस्टाग्राम - antarachoudhury.15

लिखती हैं ताकि सब पढ़ सकें।
संपर्क करने हेतु - इंस्टाग्राम - antarachoudhury.15

आँखों में ख्वाब सजाते हो ? - तुम ज़िंदा हो ...

ख्वाबों के टूट जाने डर लगता है,

डर ही है वजह जो ख्वाब देखने से रोका करता है,

दिल घबराता है , मन अशांत हो उठता है,

क्या करूँ ना करूँ यही बात सोचा करते है हम,

सवालों के घेरे में हर सवाल मुश्किल लगते है,

हारने के डर से आसान सवाल भी मुश्किलें पैदा करती है,

ख़ुशी के पल ढूंढने के खातिर

उलझनों में उलझ जाते है हमारी खुशियां

कुछ रिश्तों के बंधन में बंधकर अपनों के संग

ख्वाबों को सच करने का हौसला-अफजाई करते है जो,

साथ निभाने का वादा कर साथ निभाया करते है जो,

वही अपने ज़िन्दगी के सफलता का महत्त्व जानते है ,

और सफल होने के ख्वाबों के सफर में आखिर तक बिना सवालो के साथ निभाते है

वही होते है जिगरी यार,

कहते है जो अपने दम पर हासिल करते है, ख्वाबों को अपने हकीकत में बदलते है,

ख्वाबों को देखने के लिए चाह जगाया करते

आंखों में ख्वाबों को सजाते हो तुम ज़िंदा हो ।।